DRACULA

The Company of Monsters

DRACULA: THE COMPANY OF MONSTERS Volume Two — April 2011. Published by BOOM! Studios, a division of Boom Entertainment, Inc.

For information regarding the CPSIA on this printed material, call: (203) 595-3636 and provide reference #EAST – 71682. A catalog record of this book is available from OCLC and from the BOOM! Studios website, www.boom-studios.com, on the Librarians Page.

BOOM! Studios, 6310 San Vicente Boulevard, Suite 107, Los Angeles, CA 90048-5457. Printed in USA. First Printing. ISBN: 978-1-60886-049-4

Created and Story by:

Kurt Busiek

Written by:

Daryl Gregory

Art by:

Scott Godlewski (Chapters 5, 8)

Damian Couceiro (Chapters 6, 7)

Colors: Stephen Downer
Letters: Johnny Lowe

Cover: Ron Salas
colors: Nick Filardi

Editor: Dafna Pleban
Designer: Stephanie Gonzaga

CHAPTER 5

BARRINGTON INDUSTRIES. 12:10 AM. SATURDAY MORNING.
CORINNA?
WHAT IS IT, EVAN? IT'S AFTER MIDNIGHT.
HELP.

AN HOUR LATER.
YOU'RE SUPPOSED TO BE ABLE TO TELL YOUR FIANCÉE EVERYTHING, RIGHT?
HERE'S THE ULTIMATE TEST OF THAT: VAMPIRES ARE REAL, HONEY. *DRACULA* IS REAL.
I TELL HER HOW CONRAD AND I RESURRECTED VLAD, THEN KEPT HIM DOWN HERE.
UNTIL CONRAD DECIDED THAT HE WANTED TO BE A VAMPIRE TOO.
THAT DIDN'T GO SO WELL.
NOW MY UNCLE'S DEAD, A DRAINED HUSK. AND DRACULA HAS DISAPPEARED.

CORINNA'S TAKING THIS REMARKABLY WELL.
YOU REALLY BELIEVE ME, DON'T YOU?

YOU'VE NEVER BEEN ABLE TO LIE TO ME, EVAN.
OH, I SUPPOSE YOU *COULD* BE A HOMICIDAL MANIAC.

BUT FIVE ARMED GUARDS? *YOU?*
FRANKLY, "DRACULA DID IT" IS MORE PLAUSIBLE.
THIS IS THE VAMPIRE BLOOD?

WE'LL HAVE TO GET RID OF THAT, TOO.

DON'T BE RIDICULOUS.

SATURDAY. 4:30 PM.
STILL NO CHANGE?
I PUSHED EVERY PINT INTO HIS SYSTEM, BUT HE'S STILL A DOORNAIL.
WE NEED MORE BLOOD, THEN! HOW MUCH DID YOU USE WHEN YOU RESURRECTED DRACULA?
A LITTLE FROM ME AND CONRAD. AND 900 GALLONS OF SHEEP'S BLOOD.
DID YOU SAVE ANY?
IT'S NOT THE KIND OF THING YOU THINK YOU'RE GOING TO RE-USE.
MAYBE WE CAN USE THE BLOOD FROM THE GUARDS.
CORINNA, THEY WERE DRAINED.
PLUS, YOU ALREADY SHIPPED THEM OFF TO THE STORAGE WAREHOUSE, RIGHT?

YOU'LL HAVE TO SPREAD A RUMOR THAT THEY WENT WITH CONRAD ON ONE OF HIS MYSTERIOUS TRIPS.
EVERYONE KNOWS YOU'RE WORKING ON HIS SECRET PROJECT.
ME?
THAT'S NOT GOING TO FOOL ANYONE FOR LONG. ESPECIALLY NOT ELEANOR.
CONRAD'S SECRETARY. THE MOST ORGANIZED PERSON ON THE PLANET.
AND NOW WE HAVE TO GET RID OF CONRAD'S BODY.
YOU'RE NOT GETTING IT, EVAN. I'M AN *ACCOMPLICE* NOW.
A LIVING, BREATHING CONRAD IS THE ONLY THING THAT CAN KEEP ME OFF DEATH ROW.
AND ME.
YES, OF COURSE. BUT YOU...
...YOU HAVE TO FIND MORE BLOOD.
WHERE? ROB A BLOOD BANK?
I CAN'T DO EVERYTHING, EVAN! GET OUT THERE AND *FIND SOME!*

‹WE GOT ONE COMING OUT. IT'S NOT THE WOMAN.›*
*TRANSLATED FROM ROMANIAN.
‹WHAT DO YOU THINK OF THIS ONE'S AURA, BAS?›
‹OH, THE BOY'S BEEN JUICING. DEFINITE PERFORMANCE ENHANCERS.›
‹HEY BOSS. BAS SMELLS MAGIC ON HIM.›
‹WE'RE ROLLING.›
VROOM

SKEEEEE
CAN I HELP YOU?
HEY!
<CLEAR!>
AAH!
WHO THE HELL ARE YOU?!
CELL PHONE AND WALLET, PLEASE.
YOU'RE ROBBING ME?
AND IF I FIND A GUN ON YOU, I WILL HURT YOU.

EVAN BARRINGTON-CABOT.
<SOUNDS LIKE A JANE AUSTEN CHARACTER.>

YOUR COMPANY, BOY, HAS STOLEN ARTIFACTS FROM OUR COUNTRY.
I DON'T KNOW WHAT YOU'RE TALKING ABOUT.
STRIKE ONE!

YOU'RE LYING. YOU REEK OF SORCERY.
ARE YOU FROM THE ROMANIAN GOVERNMENT OR SOMETHING?
WE HUNT VAMPIRES, EVAN-- AND THE PEOPLE WHO RAISE VAMPIRES.
THERE'S NO SUCH THING AS--

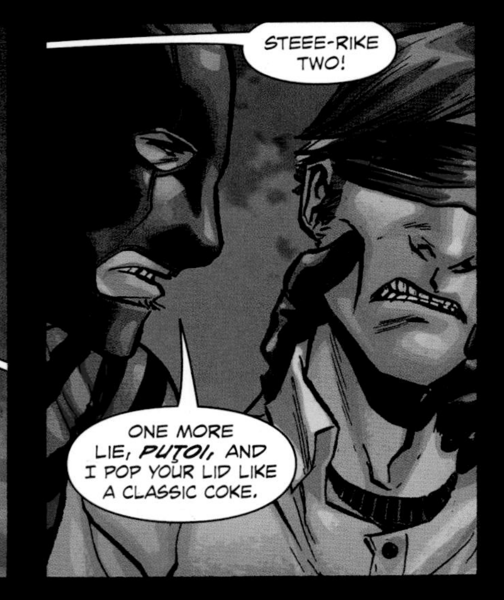

STEEE-RIKE TWO!
ONE MORE LIE, PUŢOI, AND I POP YOUR LID LIKE A CLASSIC COKE.

WHERE'S DRACULA?
I DON'T KNOW! I SWEAR!
BALL ONE.
LOOK, WE DID, UH, RESURRECT HIM. BUT HE ESCAPED. I DON'T KNOW WHERE.
WHY IN THE WORLD WOULD YOU BRING BACK SUCH A MONSTER?
WE THOUGHT WE COULD...USE HIM.
<HE'S AN IDIOT, MARTA. LET'S KILL HIM NOW.>
<NO, HE'S HIDING SOMETHING.>
<ME! ME, ME! I'LL SHOOT HIM!>
TAKE OFF YOUR BLINDFOLD, EVAN.
IF I SEE YOUR FACES, ARE YOU GOING TO KILL ME?
OFF.

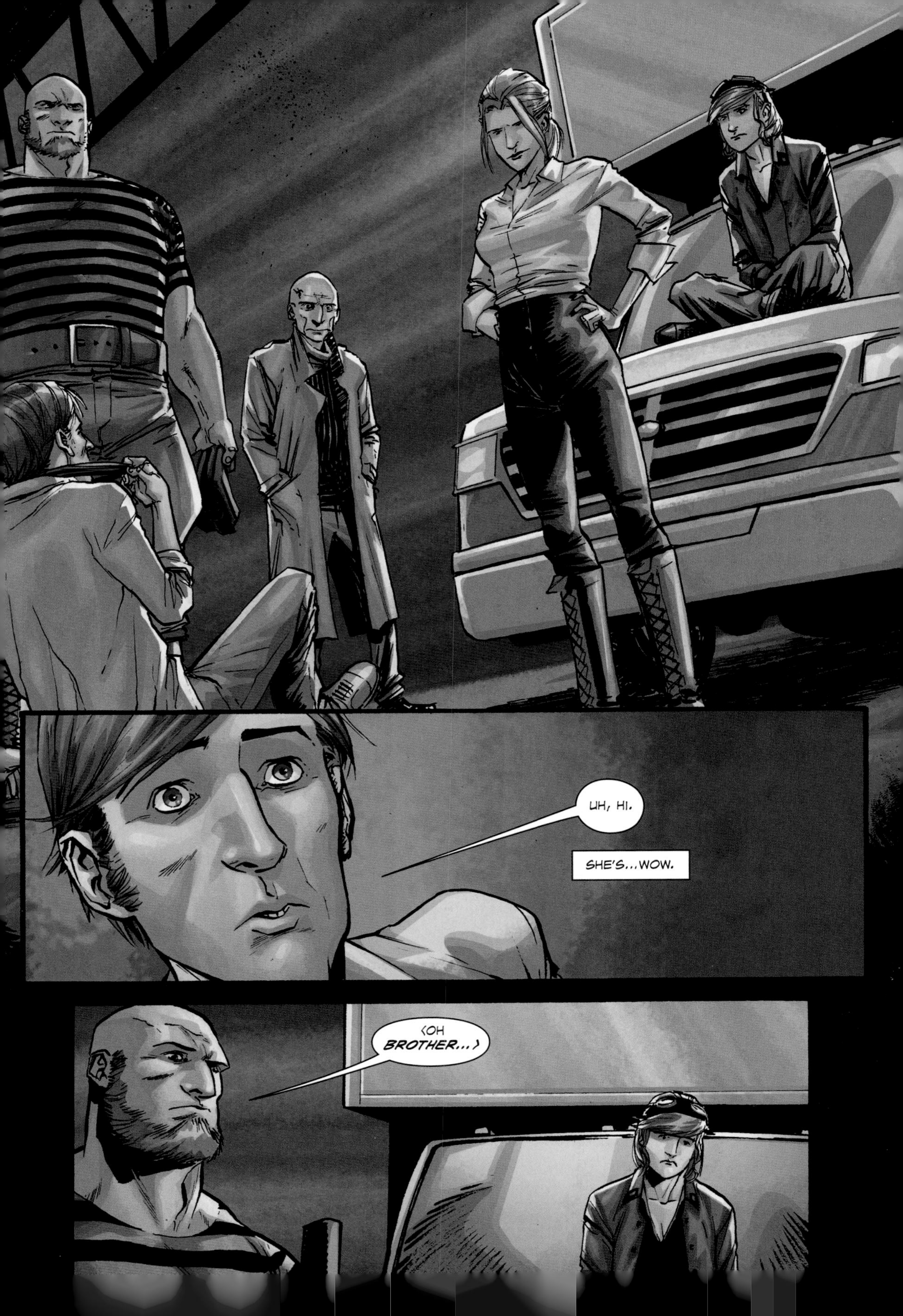
UH, HI.
SHE'S...WOW.
‹OH BROTHER...›

YOU'RE NOT AN EVIL PERSON, ARE YOU, EVAN?
BUT YOU'VE DONE A VERY BAD THING. YOU HAVE A CHANCE HERE TO... WHAT'S THE WORD IN ENGLISH?
APOLOGIZE?
BUNT!
NOT DIE.
ATONE.
WE'LL BE IN TOUCH.
YOU'RE GOING TO HELP US FIND DRACULA, EVAN.
"NO MATTER WHERE HE'S GONE TO GROUND."

SUNDAY. 11:15 PM.
I HAVE ALWAYS BELIEVED THAT THE CHURCH MISCONSTRUED THE EDEN STORY.
THE STORY OF THE FIRST SIN. OF PARADISE LOST.
CONSIDER ADAM.
NAKED AND NEW, DAMP AS CLAY. UNASHAMED.

HIS GOD GAVE HIM A MATE, AND ALLOWED HIM TO NAME THE ANIMALS.
AND THEN, THE HUMANS "SINNED."
THEIR GREAT CRIME?
EATING A PIECE OF *FRUIT.* DISOBEYING A TYRANT'S ARBITRARY LAW.
THINKING FOR THEMSELVES.
THEY HAD NOT *VIOLATED* PARADISE. THEY HAD *OUTGROWN* IT.
EXPELLED FROM THE NURSERY, THEY GAINED THE WORLD.

TO REMAKE AS THEY SAW FIT.
TO MAKE IT THEIR *HOME.*

MONDAY. 8:45 AM.
KNOCK KNOCK KNOCK
CONRAD!
MOM! ELEANOR. WHAT ARE YOU DOING HERE?
LOOKING FOR CONRAD. IS HE IN THERE WITH YOU?
NO!
EVAN, YOU LOOK TERRIBLE. WHAT DID YOU DO TO YOUR ARM?

I...I DONATED BLOOD.
HOW MUCH?
ONLY ABOUT A THOUSAND MILLILITERS. TWICE WHAT ANYBODY SHOULD GIVE IN A MONTH.
WHAT ARE YOU DOING AT B.I.? IS THERE A BOARD MEETING?
THE PEOPLE FROM VERRAMETAL ARE HERE. CONRAD IS SUPPOSED TO PRESENT THE BUYOUT OFFER.
I THOUGHT HE WAS ON A TRIP.
HIS DRIVER HASN'T SEEN HIM. THE JET IS STILL AT THE AIRPORT. AND HIS CORPORATE CARD HASN'T BEEN USED IN THREE DAYS.
HALF THE SECURITY STAFF IS MISSING TOO.
THE BUILDING'S SYSTEM WAS TURNED OFF FRIDAY NIGHT. ALARMS, CAMERAS, EVERYTHING.
WE'RE AFRAID CONRAD COULD BE KIDNAPPED.
MOM, THIS ISN'T MEXICO. WHO GETS KIDNAPPED IN PITTSBURGH?

WHO'S IN THERE WITH YOU?
NO ONE, ELEANOR. MOM, YOU KNOW HOW WE TALKED ABOUT SOME THINGS HAD TO BE KEPT SECRET FROM THE BOARD?
FINE. I'LL TALK TO THE VERRAMETAL PEOPLE, TRY TO DELAY THEM.
IF YOU HEAR *ANYTHING,* CALL ME, EVAN. I'M DEPENDING ON YOU.
BUT YOU-- YOU AREN'T ANYTHING YET.

ELEANOR'S SUSPICIOUS.
OF COURSE SHE IS.
THINK, EVAN. YOU BROUGHT BACK DRACULA, SURELY YOU CAN REVIVE--
THAT WAS DIFFERENT.
I HAD TIME, I HAD TECHNICIANS, I HAD--
TECHNICIANS? GET THEM IN HERE!
THERE WAS AN ACCIDENT. CONRAD HAD THEM CHECK ON DRACULA, AND HE...
...ATE THEM.
HUH. I DIDN'T HEAR A PEEP IN H.R. ABOUT ANY MISSING EMPLOYEES.
THEY WERE INTERNS.
OH. NO WONDER.
WHAT ARE WE GOING TO DO ABOUT ELEANOR? IF SHE CALLS THE COPS...
I'LL GET HER ON OUR SIDE.
YOU WATCH CONRAD. I'LL BE BACK BY NIGHTFALL.

MONDAY. 8:00 PM.
...BECAUSE YOU KNOW MORE ABOUT THIS COMPANY THAN ANYONE--PROBABLY EVEN CONRAD.
NOT QUITE. CONRAD NEVER SHARED THE DETAILS OF THIS LITTLE SIDE PROJECT OF HIS.
DEEP. DEEP-DEEP-DEEP
WHAT I DON'T UNDERSTAND IS WHY HE INVOLVED HIS NEPHEW AND A MIDDLE MANAGER FROM HUMAN RESOURCES.
BUT THAT'S RIGHT--YOU'RE EVAN'S *FIANCÉE?*
ONCE YOU SEE WHAT WE'VE BEEN WORKING ON, YOU'LL UNDERSTAND EVERYTHING.
AND WHY WE NEED YOUR HELP.
OH MY GOD.

IT'S NOT AS BAD AS IT LOOKS.
WHAT?
AAAH!
CORINNA!
ELEANOR...

WELCOME BACK, CONRAD.
GOOD TO *BE* BACK.

CHAPTER 6

2:30 AM.
ACCESSORY TO MURDER.

WHEN JUST PLAIN MURDER ISN'T ENOUGH, CONSIDER THIS HANDY CARRYING CASE AND FREE A.C. ADAPTER.
WHAT NO ONE TELLS YOU WHEN YOU FIRST GET INTO THE ACCESSORY BUSINESS, IS HOW LONG THE NIGHTS ARE.

YOU POP YOUR NEMBUTAL AND ATIVAN AND AMBIEN. YOU STARE AT THE CEILING.
AND YOU KNOW YOU'RE ABSOLUTELY ALONE.

GOOD EVENING, APPRENTICE.

GAH!

GET BACK!
YOU'RE SLEEPING WITH A CROSS?
MY.
ARE YOU A *CHRISTIAN,* EVAN?

I...BELIEVE IN GOD.
YOU DON'T SOUND VERY SURE.
NOW PLEASE, PUT THE TRINKET AWAY. THE ICON PAINS ME, AND WE HAVE ***BUSINESS*** TO DISCUSS.
YOU'RE NOT HERE TO KILL ME? YOUR PAROLE STILL HOLDS?

FOR YOU.
YOUR UNCLE, HOWEVER, HAS BROKEN HIS WORD TO ME.
I SPARED HIS LIFE ONCE, OUT OF DEFERENCE TO MY OATH TO YOU. BUT NOW...

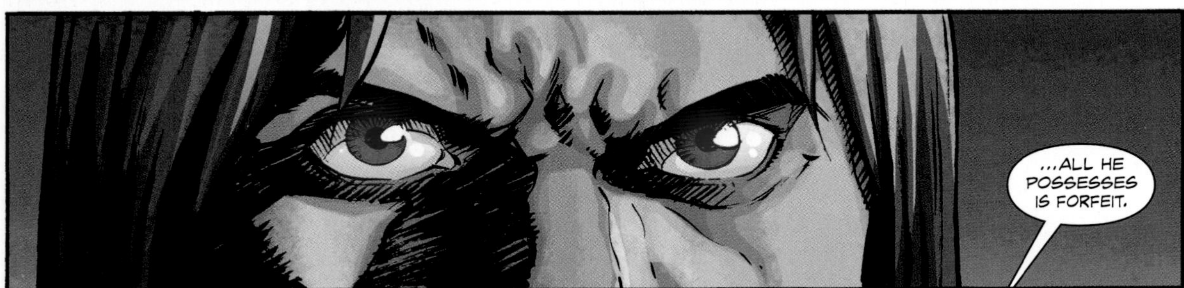
...ALL HE POSSESSES IS FORFEIT.

IT'S JUST THAT IT'S BEEN TWO WEEKS.
I THOUGHT YOU'D BE GONE BY NOW. BACK TO YOUR HOMELAND.
I'VE DECIDED TO MAKE AMERICA MY HOME.

I KNOW WHAT YOU'RE THINKING--ANOTHER ILLEGAL IMMIGRANT TAKING A JOB AWAY FROM SOME HARDWORKING AMERICAN.

ON THE CONTRARY, I AM HERE TO OFFER YOU A POSITION. CALL IT DAY MANAGER.

YOU WILL OF COURSE BE HANDSOMELY COMPENSATED.
AND YOU WILL BE FREE TO RUN BARRINGTON INDUSTRIES AS YOU WISH.

RUN B.I.--ME?

MOST IMPORTANTLY, YOU WILL BECOME MY APPRENTICE.
THE SECRETS OF THE SCHOLOMANCE WILL BE YOURS.
HOWEVER...

...IF YOU CAST YOUR LOT WITH CONRAD, YOU WILL SHARE HIS FATE.
IS THAT UNDERSTOOD?
BUT...

I AWAIT YOUR DECISION.

BARRINGTON INDUSTRIES.
COULD YOU PLEASE PAGE MR. BARRINGTON?
THEY'VE BEEN GONE FOR OVER AN HOUR. IF THEY'VE LEFT THE BUILDING...

YOU HAVE TO LET THE BIG BOYS TALK ON THEIR OWN.
THEY'RE PROBABLY COMING TO AN AGREEMENT RIGHT NOW.

AGREEMENT? I DON'T THINK SO. WE'VE BEEN AT THIS FOR HOURS, AND IT'S CLEAR THAT B.I. IS ON THE ROCKS.
YOU NEED VERRAMETAL MORE THAN WE NEED YOU.

BUT *WE* HAVE THE *CASH.*

ONLY BECAUSE YOU'VE TRADED LONG-TERM CAPACITY FOR A SHORT-TERM ADVANTAGE.
YOU'VE LAID OFF THOUSANDS OF PEOPLE AND SHUT DOWN HALF YOUR MANUFACTURING.

AND YOU STILL DON'T HAVE ENOUGH MONEY TO *FORCE* A BUYOUT.
WHEN MR. BARRINGTON AND MR. LEWIS COME BACK, I'M GOING TO RECOMMEND--

GOOD NEWS, EVERYONE!

RON AND I HAVE WORKED EVERYTHING OUT.
WE'VE WORKED EVERYTHING OUT.

MR. LEWIS, I HOPE YOU HAVEN'T--
CLEAR SYNERGIES. WIN-WIN. MAXIMIZED STOCKHOLDER VALUE.

WE'LL HAVE THE LAWYERS DRAW UP THE PAPERS, AND WE'LL DO THE FINAL SIGNING IN, SAY, TWO WEEKS?

THAT'S... THAT'S...
PERFECT.

COULDN'T HAVE SAID IT BETTER MYSELF.

HALF AN HOUR LATER.
CUZ!

WHAT ARE YOU DOING HERE?
OH, NOTHING MUCH.
JUST SAVING THE COMPANY.

YOU GUYS SEEM... AWAKE.
WE'RE HEADING OUT TO CELEBRATE. I'D INVITE YOU, BUT I DON'T THINK IT'D BE TO YOUR TASTE.
NO OFFENSE.

I'M, UH, LOOKING FOR CORINNA. IS SHE INSIDE?
CHECK CONRAD'S OFFICE.

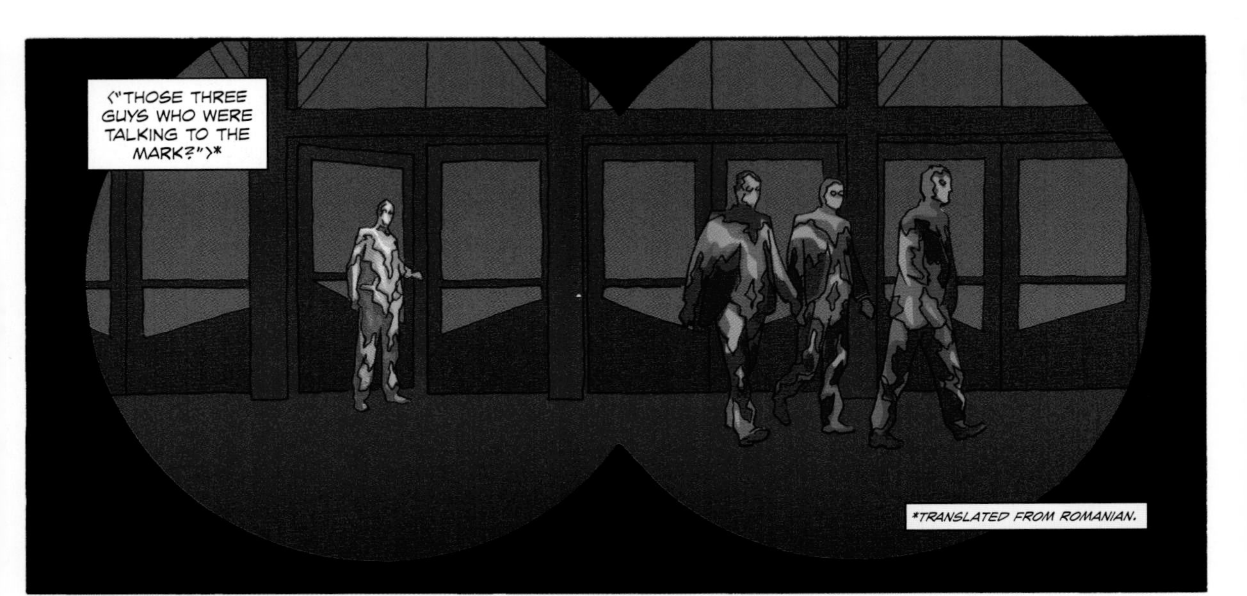

<"THOSE THREE GUYS WHO WERE TALKING TO THE MARK?">*
*TRANSLATED FROM ROMANIAN.

<YEAH?>
<SEVERE BODY HEAT DEFICIENCY.>

<ALL *THREE* OF THEM?>
<THEY'RE GETTING INTO THEIR CARS.>

<HMMM. STAY WITH THE RICH BOY, OR FOLLOW THE VERMIN?>
<VERMIN VERMIN VERMIN!>

<CALL THE BOSS.>

CORINNA? TORRENCE SAID YOU WERE...

...UP HERE.

EVAN! YOU MISSED THE EXCITEMENT.
VERRAMETAL IS OURS FOR THE TAKING.

THAT'S... GREAT.
YOU LOOK UPSET. IS SOMETHING BOTHERING YOU?

I JUST SAW TORRENCE, RYAN, AND SEAN.
YES?

YOU TURNED THEM INTO *VAMPIRES!*

THEY WERE UP FOR PROMOTION.
CONRAD, YOU CAN'T GO AROUND MAKING--

I *CAN'T?* I ***CAN'T?***

AAAH!

HOW DARE YOU...
CONRAD, YOU HAVE TO GET AHOLD OF YOURSELF.
DRACULA IS STILL OUT THERE. HE'S WATCHING.

YOU SAID HE LEFT.
HE CAME TO...WARN YOU.
NO, EVAN. WARN US.

I'M OUT, CONRAD. DONE. YOU DON'T NEED ME ANYMORE.

OH, EVAN. YOU HAVE NO IDEA HOW VALUABLE YOU ARE. YOU'RE MY COURT MAGICIAN.
AND WE BOTH KNOW YOU HAVE NOWHERE TO RUN.

YOU WILL USE YOUR TALENTS, EVAN. FIND DRACULA-- AND BRING HIM TO ME.

EXCUSE ME, I'D LIKE TO GIVE YOU MY ORGAN DONOR CARD.
I BEG YOUR PARDON?

YOU MIGHT AS WELL TAKE ALL OF ME...

...BECAUSE YOU ALREADY HAVE MY HEART.

AH. A *PICK UP* LINE.
WELL, MR. SENIOR MARKETING REP. FROM BARRINGTON INDUSTRIES...

...I WAS JUST LEAVING.
LET ME WALK YOU TO YOUR CAR.

I LOVE YOUR ACCENT. WHERE ARE YOU FROM?
IOWA.
EXIT

‹...LOOKS LIKE HE'S GOING TO USE A NINE-IRON...›
MY CAR IS RIGHT DOWN THIS ALLEY.
GOOD THING I'M HERE WITH YOU.
THE BITE

THIS CAN BE A ROUGH NEIGHBORHOOD.

SO I'VE HEARD.

YOU'RE TRYING TO *ROB* ME?
NOT EXACTLY.

KRA-ACK!

WHERE IS YOUR MASTER, VERMIN?
WHO, CONRAD? I DON'T KNOW-- AT WORK?

NOT YOUR *BOSS.* YOUR VAMPIRE MASTER--THE ONE WHO MADE YOU.
DRACULA, IMBECILE.

DRACULA? NEVER MET THE GUY. CONRAD SAID HE *RAN AWAY.*
WHO BIT YOU THEN?
I TOLD YOU--CONRAD! CONRAD BARRINGTON!

WE'VE BEEN LIED TO.

KILL THIS VERMIN.
WHO ARE YOU TALKING TO?

THE SIXTEEN-YEAR-OLD GIRL ON THE ROOF.

OH YEAH, WHAT'S ***SHE*** SUPPOSED TO--

BLAM

WHAT IS IT?
RYAN IS... DEAD.

SKREEE!
WHY DID YOU STOP? I WANT TO BE HOME BY DAWN!
I'M SORRY, SIR...

"...THERE'S SOMEONE IN THE ROAD."

YOU KILLED ONE OF MY VAMPIRES.
YOU'VE LOST ONE OF YOUR CHILDREN? MY CONDOLENCES.
YOU ARE LOOKING WELL, HOWEVER. HOW ARE YOU ENJOYING MY BLOOD?

WHAT DO YOU WANT?

YOUR WEALTH, YOUR SHARES IN B.I., YOUR HOMES, YOUR LANDS.
YOUR KINGDOM.

TURN THEM OVER AND I WILL ALLOW YOUR REMAINING OFFSPRING TO SURVIVE...
...AS MY SERVANTS.

GO TO HELL!

THAT WOULD BE NO, THEN? YOU'VE BEEN WARNED.

MIST? HE CAN TURN TO MIST?
I WANT THAT!

THAT WAS HIM?
WOW.

NEW STRATEGY.
YOU'RE IN HUMAN RESOURCES, AREN'T YOU?

FIND ME SOME HUMANS.

CHAPTER 7

I KNOW MANY OF YOU THINK I'M A VILLAIN.

I'M THE MAN WHO TOOK YOUR JOB AWAY FROM YOU.
THEN I SENT YOU OUT INTO THE WORST ECONOMY SINCE THE GREAT DEPRESSION.

I WILL NOT APOLOGIZE FOR THAT.

THIS COMPANY, MY FAMILY'S COMPANY, WAS ABOUT TO GO UNDER.
I DID WHAT I HAD TO DO.
BUT *BECAUSE* I TOOK THOSE STEPS, I AM NOW IN A POSITION TO TELL YOU THIS...

WELCOME BACK.

CLAP CLAP
WOOT!
CLAP
CLAP CLAP CLAP
CLAP CLAP CLAP CLAP CLAP
CLAP CLAP CLAP

PLEASE. I APPLAUD YOU.
YOU'VE BEEN SPECIALLY CHOSEN.
YOU'RE YOUNG, WITHOUT FAMILIES TO TIE YOU DOWN...
...AND MOST IMPORTANTLY, AMBITIOUS.

YOU DESERVE THIS SECOND CHANCE.
CORINNA?

GOOD EVENING, EVERYONE.
IF YOU'LL OPEN YOUR ORIENTATION PACKETS?

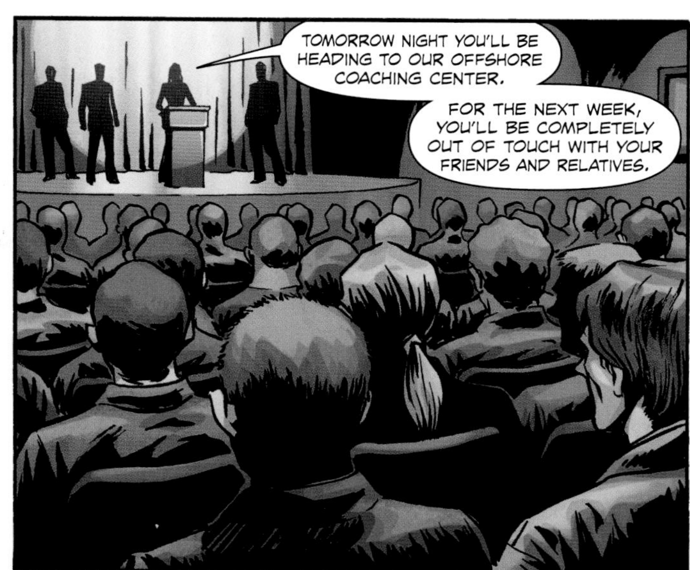
TOMORROW NIGHT YOU'LL BE HEADING TO OUR OFFSHORE COACHING CENTER.
FOR THE NEXT WEEK, YOU'LL BE COMPLETELY OUT OF TOUCH WITH YOUR FRIENDS AND RELATIVES.

AS YOU KNOW FROM THE CONTRACT AND N.D.A. YOU SIGNED, THIS PROJECT IS TOP SECRET.
YOU'LL UNDERGO INTENSIVE TRAINING FOR YOUR NEW POSITIONS.

I CAN'T EVEN TELL YOU WHAT THAT TRAINING ENTAILS.
BUT I GUARANTEE THAT YOU WILL LEARN ONE THING...

...THERE IS LIFE AFTER TERMINATION.

THURSDAY.
5:30 PM.

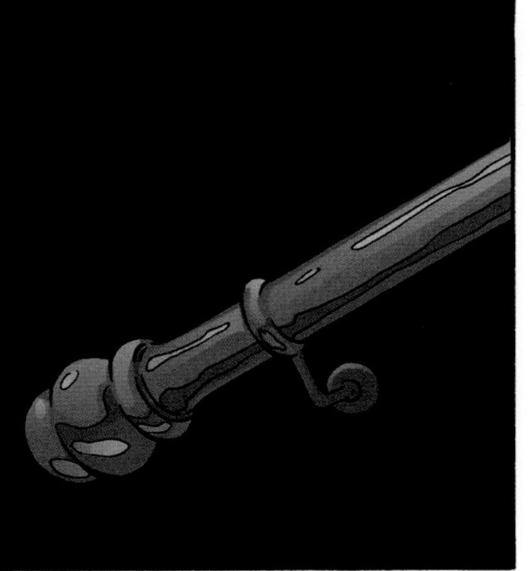

MARTA!
WHAT ARE YOU--

GOING SOMEWHERE, EVAN?

WHAT ARE YOU TALKING ABOUT? AND DOESN'T ANYBODY KNOCK ANYMORE?
YOUR BAGS ARE PACKED. YOU WEREN'T GOING TO SKIP TOWN BEFORE YOU TOLD US ABOUT YOUR UNCLE, WERE YOU?
YOU KNOW, THE ONE WHO'S A VAMPIRE?
OH.
LOOK, HE WASN'T A VAMPIRE YET WHEN I TALKED TO YOU. HE WAS JUST...DEAD.
IT TOOK AWHILE AFTER WE MADE DRACULA BITE HIM.

YOU MADE DRACULA TURN HIM?
CONRAD GOT TIRED OF WAITING. I TOLD YOU, WE THOUGHT WE'D BE ABLE TO MAKE DRACULA WORK FOR US--

NO ONE CONTROLS DRACULA.
SEE, THAT'S WHY WE USED OUR OWN BLOOD TO RAISE HIM, SO HE COULDN'T CONTROL US, BUT THEN--

STOP! YOU DID WHAT?
IT WAS IN THE CRUENTUS PACTUM. BUT WHEN THAT DIDN'T WORK--
YOU HAVE THE PACTUM? DO YOU REALIZE WHAT YOU'VE DONE?

OLD PLAYBOOK! AMERICAN LEAGUE!
‹THESE MORONS HAVE STARTED A NEW PYRAMID.›*
*TRANSLATED FROM ROMANIAN.

ALL POWER FLOWS *DOWN,* EVAN. WHEN DRACULA WAS DEAD, HIS CHILDREN WERE WEAK, FEEBLE THINGS.
AS SOON AS YOU BROUGHT HIM BACK, THEY BECAME REJUVENATED. ***AGGRESSIVE.***
AND A GREAT MAN DIED.

NOW YOU'RE TELLING ME THAT CONRAD HAS HIS OWN POWER SUPPLY.
HOW MANY OTHER VAMPIRES HAS HE MADE?
ONLY TWO MORE.
THAT I KNOW OF.

AND HOW MANY CHILDREN HAVE ***THEY*** MADE?
I DON'T KNOW!

THIS IS A NEW ARMY, EVAN! ANYONE CONRAD TURNS, HE ***CONTROLS.*** AND THAT'S AN ARMY DRACULA DOESN'T COMMAND.
YOU'VE SINGLE-HANDEDLY DOUBLED THE WORLD'S VAMPIRE PROBLEM.

‹UNBELIEVABLE.›
‹I KNOW! PIRATES ACTUALLY WORSE THAN CUBS.›

DRACULA WANTS CONRAD. WE WANT DRACULA.
SO THIS IS WHAT'S GOING TO HAPPEN.

FIRST, YOU'RE GOING TO TURN OVER EVERYTHING FROM THE SCHOLOMANCE, STARTING WITH THE PACTUM.
AND SECOND--
LEAD YOU TO CONRAD. I GET IT.

YOU KNOW, ABOUT A WEEK AGO, YOU WERE ALL VERY INTIMIDATING.
BUT SINCE THEN? I'VE WATCHED DRACULA TEAR APART HALF A DOZEN PEOPLE.
SO THIS IS THE NEW DEAL.

CONRAD'S HOLED UP. THE SCHOLOMANCE MATERIAL IS LOCKED AWAY.
WITHOUT ME, YOU DON'T GET THE PACTUM, YOU DON'T GET CONRAD...
AND YOU SURE AS HELL DON'T GET DRACULA.

<IS THIS IDIOT TRYING TO NEGOTIATE?>
<THIS IDIOT ALSO SPEAKS ROMANIAN. AND *YES.*>
HA!

I LIKE IT WHEN YOU'RE...WHAT'S THE WORD? ***SPUNKY.***
WHAT DO YOU WANT IN RETURN?
PROTECTION. WHEN THE VAMPIRES COME FOR ME, YOU TAKE THEM OUT.
YOU ***ARE*** VAMPIRE KILLERS, RIGHT?

FINE. LET'S GO, COUSINS.
AS FOR YOU, BRING US THE BOOK AND CONRAD, AND WE HAVE A DEAL.
MY NUMBER IS ON YOUR CELL.

REMEMBER, SLUGGER. WHEN YOU PLAY WITH THE BOOK...

...THE BOOK ALSO PLAYS ***YOU.***

1471. LAKE HERMANNSTADT.
THE SCHOLOMANCE.
THE PAGE IS OPEN, BASARAB.
PRINCE, THIS BINDS YOU TO PREPARE THE WAY FOR...FOR THE *END* OF THE *WORLD.*
THE THINGS THIS PACT REQUIRES ARE... ***UNSPEAKABLE.***
YET YOU ***WILL*** SPEAK IT.

PRINCE! MY PRINCE!

PRINCE?

FRIDAY. 10:00 AM.
THE BOOK IS MY INSURANCE POLICY.

TOO DANGEROUS TO LEAVE WITH CONRAD, AND TOO VALUABLE TO JUST HAND OVER TO MARTA.
MY ONLY WEAPON.
EVAN! IT LOOKS LIKE YOU'RE MOVING BACK IN.

NO, I'M JUST...IS IT OKAY IF I STORE SOME STUFF HERE? MY APARTMENT IS...
CONSTANTLY BEING BROKEN INTO.
...A LITTLE CROWDED.

OF COURSE.
I'VE GOT TO RUN TO THE OFFICE FOR AN EMERGENCY BOARD MEETING, BUT ADELE WILL BE HERE IF YOU NEED ANYTHING.

IS THERE A PROBLEM?
WE HAVE A HUNDRED PROBLEMS, BUT THIS MAY BE A SOLUTION TO THE BIGGEST ONE.
WHAT IS THIS?

NOTHING. JUST RESEARCH.
YOUR FATHER WAS OBSESSED WITH OLD BOOKS. GERMAN, LATIN, ROMANIAN...
REALLY? I DIDN'T KNOW THAT.

I JUST HOPE THAT YOU'RE NOT...FOLLOWING HIS FOOTSTEPS.
YOU MEAN GOING *INSANE?*

YOUR FATHER WAS *ILL.* I KNOW YOU'RE NOT HIM, BUT I *AM* WORRIED ABOUT YOU.
ARE YOU ALL RIGHT? I CAN POSTPONE THE MEETING.

THIS IS THE TIME TO TELL HER I'M LEAVING.
DON'T WORRY, MOM.

ALL THAT'S LEFT IS TO TALK TO CORINNA AND FIND OUT IF I'M GOING ALONE.
GO TO YOUR MEETING.
I'M FINE.

I REALLY MUST OBJECT, MARGARET.

WE AGREED THAT THE VERRAMETAL DEAL WILL BE READY TO SIGN MONDAY NIGHT.
I CAN'T DROP EVERYTHING I'M WORKING ON AND BE THERE IN THE MIDDLE OF THE DAY.

WE'VE RECEIVED A BUYOUT OFFER, CONRAD. A SUBSTANTIAL OFFER.
I FIND THAT HARD TO BELIEVE. WHO IS THIS OFFER FROM?

AN EASTERN EUROPEAN INVESTMENT FIRM CALLED THE HERMANNSTADT GROUP.
HAVE YOU HEARD OF IT?

CONRAD? ARE YOU THERE?

EXCUSE ME. MY SCREEN SEEMS TO HAVE *BROKEN.*

I'LL EXPRESS MAIL THE PAPERS TO YOUR HOUSE. THEY'RE OFFERING NEARLY FOUR TIMES WHAT--
NO.

CONRAD, IT'S THE BOARD'S RESPONSIBILITY TO--
THIS IS OUR *HERITAGE,* MARGARET. OUR *FAMILY NAME.*

I LOVE B.I. MORE THAN ANYONE. BUT YOUR MANEUVERS HAVE PUT THE ENTIRE COMPANY AT RISK.
WE HAVE TO CONSIDER THE THOUSANDS OF EMPLOYEES WHO DEPEND ON US.
HERMANNSTADT IS GUARANTEEING TO RE-OPEN THE OHIO PLANTS, CONRAD.
4,500 PEOPLE REHIRED! I DON'T THINK YOU UNDERSTAND HOW--
NO, YOU DON'T UNDERSTAND. THIS IS BARRINGTON INDUSTRIES.
WE WILL NOT BE OWNED BY ANYONE, CERTAINLY NOT... EUROPEANS.
WE WILL MEET MONDAY NIGHT, AS SCHEDULED.
I AM CONFIDENT THAT BY THEN THIS BOARD WILL DECIDE TO REJECT THIS BUYOUT OFFER...
...AND APPROVE OUR PURCHASE OF VERRAMETAL.

SUNDAY. 8:45 PM.
ULTIMATUM TIME.

CORINNA'S FLIGHT ARRIVES IN AN HOUR.
I HAVE TO TALK TO HER BEFORE SHE CAN SEE CONRAD.

MAKE HER TELL ME WHOSE SIDE SHE'S ON. IS SHE STAYING WITH CONRAD, OR COMING WITH--
EVAN BARRINGTON-CABOT?

UH...WHO?

I THINK YOU'VE GOT THE WRONG GUY.

I DON'T THINK SO.
I'VE BROUGHT YOU YOUR CONTRACT. GENTLEMEN?

WHO ARE THESE GUYS--A COUPLE OF YOUR SOULLESS MINIONS?

YES. I CALL THEM *LAWYERS.*
AS FUTURE C.E.O., I FELT YOU SHOULD BE NOTIFIED THAT MY PURCHASE OF BARRINGTON INDUSTRIES HAS BEGUN.

THIS MUCH CASH...HOW IS THAT POSSIBLE? WHAT KIND OF MAGIC HAVE YOU USED TO--
THE DARK ART OF *ANATOCISM,* EVAN.

I...I DON'T KNOW WHAT THAT IS.
PERHAPS YOU KNOW IT BY ITS MORE COMMON NAME--COMPOUND INTEREST.
I HAVE HAD FUNDS INVESTED FOR CENTURIES. I TAKE...THE LONG VIEW.

B.I. IS A PRIVATE COMPANY. THE BOARD WILL NEVER AGREE TO A BUYOUT.
HAS CONRAD TAUGHT YOU NOTHING? BOARD MEMBERS CAN BE MANIPULATED.
EVEN RECALCITRANT CHAIRWOMEN CAN BE REMOVED.

YOU BASTARD! ARE YOU THREATENING--?

I THREATEN NOTHING.
PERHAPS YOU SHOULD VISIT YOUR MOTHER.

AS SOON AS I SEE THAT THE DOOR IS AJAR, I KNOW IT IN MY BONES.
I'M TOO LATE.
THE MONSTER HAS BEEN IN THE HOUSE.
RTSON
TERING
ADELE!
I'VE KNOWN HER MY ENTIRE LIFE. SHE WAS MY FIRST BABYSITTER. FIRST COMPANION.
FIRST FRIEND.

THIS ONE'S A STRANGER. ONE OF THE CATERERS, EVIDENTLY.
ANOTHER SERVANT IN THE WRONG PLACE WHEN THE MONSTER CAME.

AND THEN I REALIZE MY MISTAKE.

THE MONSTER IS STILL HERE.
EVAN! THANK GOODNESS YOU'RE HERE.
I ORDERED OUT, BUT I'M STILL *FAMISHED.*

CHAPTER 8

COME GIVE MOMMY A KISS.
HE GOT TO HER. DRACULA GOT TO HER.
OH GOD, OH GOD...
AAAGH!

I CAN'T TELL YOU HOW GOOD IT FEELS TO GET OUT OF THAT DAMN CHAIR.
THE MOST ANNOYING THING? ALWAYS LOOKING UP AT EVERYONE.
GNNN.
HISSSSS!
MANNERS!

WHY ARE YOU BEING DIFFICULT?
YOU WERE ALWAYS SUCH AN *OBEDIENT* CHILD.
AAAAAGH!
GAH!
THE DAMN *DOG* TASTES BETTER THAN YOU!
WHAT'S THE MATTER WITH YOUR *BLOOD?*
MY BLOOD IS IN DRACULA. AND DRACULA'S IS IN HER. *FEEDBACK LOOP.*
GET OUT OF HERE, EVAN. FIND ME SOME *REAL* FOOD.

HOLD ON.
HOLD ON.
HOLD ON.
HOLD...
AAAAH!
CORINNA.
HER FLIGHT IS COMING IN ANY MINUTE. SHE'LL KNOW WHAT TO DO.

CORINNA ALWAYS KNOWS WHAT TO DO.
SHE'S A *SURVIVOR.*

SHE GREW UP IN SOUTH CAROLINA, ON THE KNIFE-EDGE OF POVERTY.
A MAN SHE TRUSTED DID BAD THINGS TO HER.

AND KEPT DOING THEM.

CORINNA! *CORINNA!*

TORRENCE, TELL THE OTHERS TO BAG UP THE FLIGHT ATTENDANTS AND GET IN THE CARS. WE'LL BE LATE.
EVAN HAS COME OUT IN THE RAIN TO MEET ME.
ISN'T THAT SWEET.
THE NIGHT SHE TOLD ME WAS THE FIRST AND LAST TIME I SAW HER CRY. BUT IT WAS ENOUGH.
SHE TRUSTED ME. SHE CHOSE ME.
AND NOW WE CAN FIND A WAY OUT OF THIS MESS, TOGETHER.
SOMETHING TERRIBLE'S HAPPENED TO MY MOTHER.
SHE ATTACKED ME, AND--
CORINNA? ARE YOU ALL RIGHT?
ME? I'M FANTASTIC.
DAMN IT!
WHO DID THIS TO YOU? CONRAD?
YOU DON'T GET IT.
I VOLUNTEERED.
SNAP!

IT'S FINALLY COMING TOGETHER FOR ME, EVAN.
CONRAD NEEDS ME.
I'M TEMPTED TO BRING YOU OVER TO THE TEAM, EVAN.
BUT IT LOOKS LIKE SOMEONE ALREADY TRIED.
BESIDES, CONRAD VETOED TURNING YOU. GOD KNOWS WHY, CUZ.
WHAT'S YOUR RESEARCH DONE FOR US LATELY?
MAYBE IT'S FOR THE BEST. WE'VE...GROWN APART.
I'M SORRY, EVAN...
...BUT IT'S TIME TO MOVE ON.

MONDAY. 8:15 AM.
EVERY PROMISE IS EVENTUALLY BROKEN.

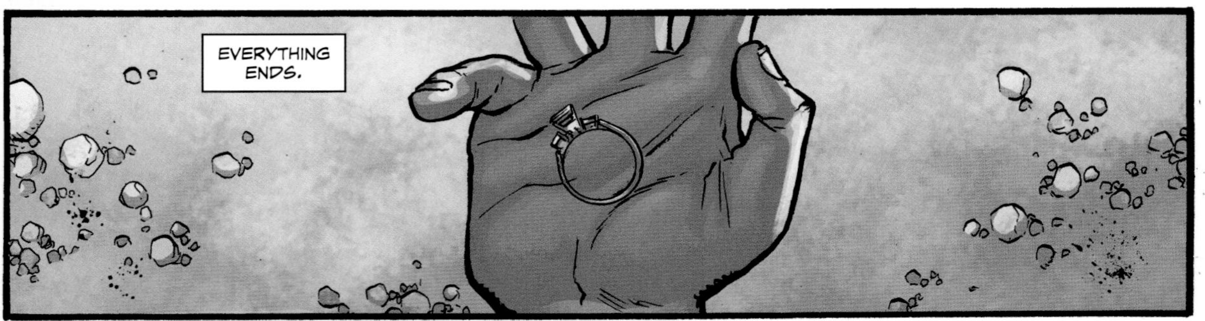
EVERYTHING ENDS.

EVERYTHING DIES.
PLOP
AT LEAST, EVERYTHING IS SUPPOSED TO.

WHEN THE DEAD COME BACK, THEY MAKE DEMANDS. OFFERS YOU CAN'T REFUSE.
DRACULA WANTS ME TO BE HIS DAY MANAGER--THE HUMAN FIGUREHEAD OF HIS NEW COMPANY.
IF THE BOARD APPROVES THE BUYOUT, CONRAD AND THE COUSINS ARE OUT. AND I'M IN. INSTANT C.E.O.
AND PAWN TO THE CREATURE WHO TURNED MY MOTHER.
IT LOOKS LIKE MERCURY, ONE OF PARACELSUS' TRIA PRIMA.
THE PRINCIPLE OF TRANSFORMATION, JOINING THE HIGH TO THE LOW.
AN ALCHEMICAL IN-JOKE FROM A SORCERER TO HIS PROSPECTIVE APPRENTICE.
BUT THE SYMBOL IS INCOMPLETE.
FINISH IT, AND I'LL HAVE SIGNED THE CONTRACT AND PASSED MY FIRST TEST.
WHAT DO YOU HAVE THERE, MR. BARRINGTON-CABOT?

DAMN IT! DO YOU HAVE TO FOLLOW ME EVERYWHERE?
MARTA ŞTEFĂNESCU. ROMANIAN VAMPIRE KILLER.
SO WHERE'S THE REST OF THE TEAM? FRED, SHAGGY...?
THIS LOGO--IT'S THE ORDER OF THE DRAGON.
WHAT IS DRACULA UP TO?
HE'S FORMED A COMPANY CALLED THE HERMANNSTADT GROUP. HE'S TRYING TO BUY OUT B.I.
DRACULA IS IN BUSINESS?
NOW THAT IS FRIGHTENING.
I'M WORRIED ABOUT YOU, EVAN.
YOU HAVEN'T WRITTEN, YOU HAVEN'T CALLED.
AND THERE'S A BANDAGE ON YOUR NECK.
ONE OF THE NEW VAMPIRES TRIED TO NIP ME. DON'T WORRY, THEY DIDN'T GET ANY BLOOD.
FINE, KEEP YOUR SECRETS.
YOU'RE NOT BACKING OUT ON OUR DEAL, ARE YOU?

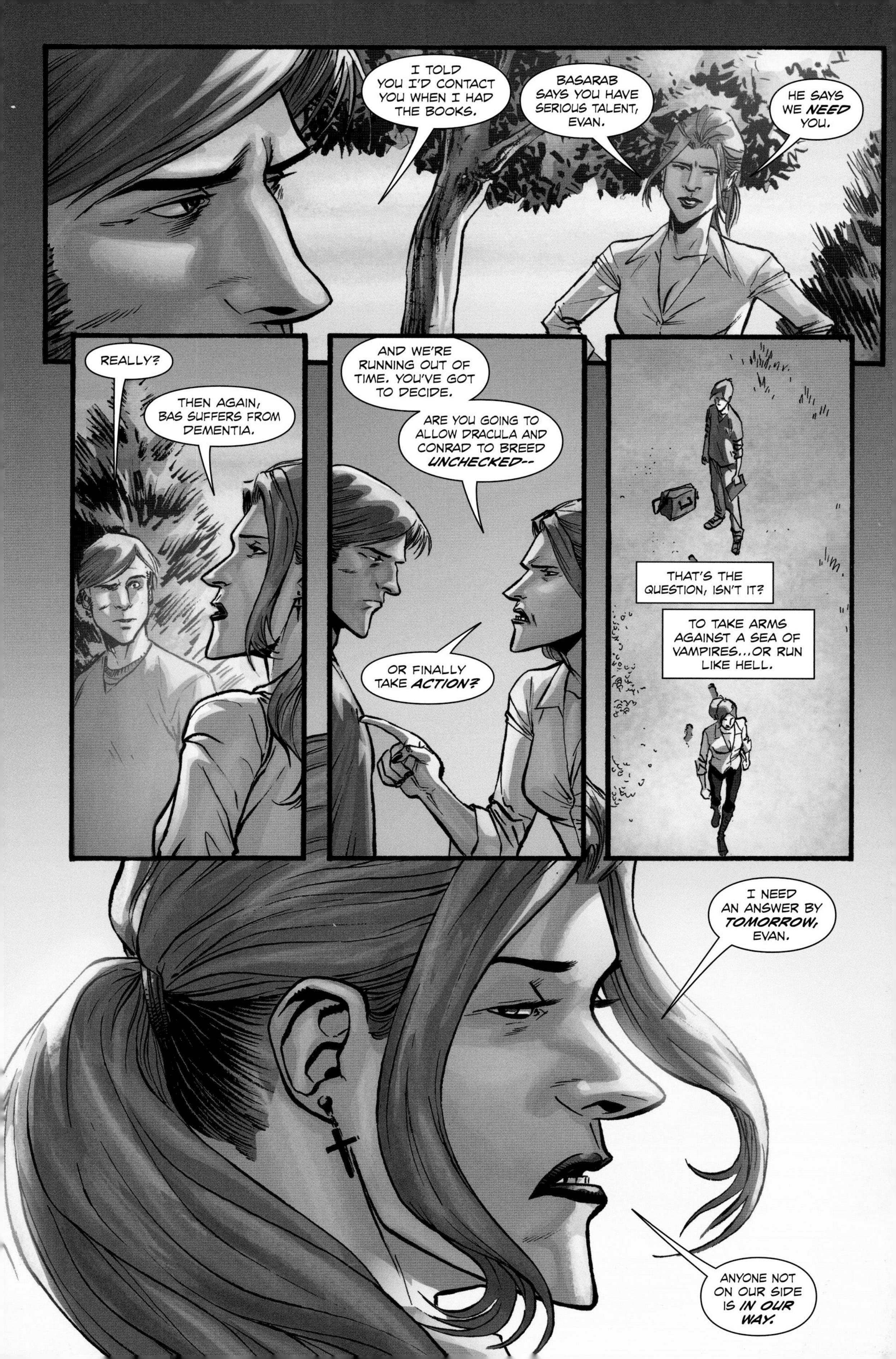
I TOLD YOU I'D CONTACT YOU WHEN I HAD THE BOOKS.
BASARAB SAYS YOU HAVE SERIOUS TALENT, EVAN.
HE SAYS WE *NEED* YOU.
REALLY?
THEN AGAIN, BAS SUFFERS FROM DEMENTIA.
AND WE'RE RUNNING OUT OF TIME. YOU'VE GOT TO DECIDE.
ARE YOU GOING TO ALLOW DRACULA AND CONRAD TO BREED *UNCHECKED*--
OR FINALLY TAKE *ACTION?*
THAT'S THE QUESTION, ISN'T IT?
TO TAKE ARMS AGAINST A SEA OF VAMPIRES...OR RUN LIKE HELL.
I NEED AN ANSWER BY *TOMORROW,* EVAN.
ANYONE NOT ON OUR SIDE IS *IN OUR WAY.*

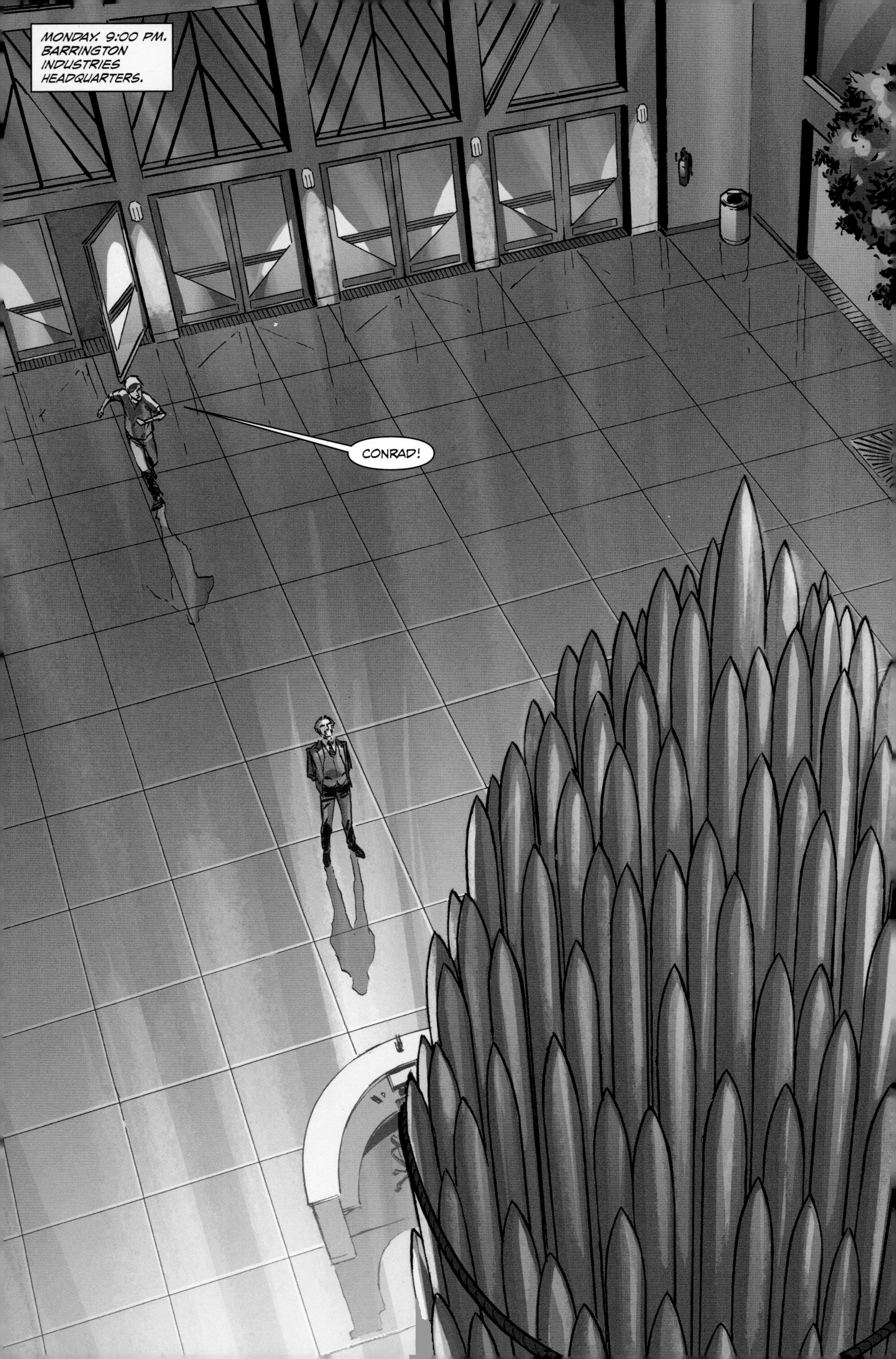
MONDAY. 9:00 PM.
BARRINGTON
INDUSTRIES
HEADQUARTERS.
CONRAD!

I HAVE TO TALK TO YOU ABOUT DRACULA. HE--
WHEN WE INSTALLED THIS SCULPTURE, YOUR FATHER CALLED IT *FASCIST.*
WHAT *IS* IT THAT YOU'RE SO UPSET ABOUT? THE BOARD IS WAITING FOR ME.
AH. I KNOW. CORINNA SAID YOU WERE UPSET WITH HER *LIFESTYLE* CHOICE.
SAID IT LOOKED LIKE THEIR SYMBOL--A BUNDLE OF STICKS.
GOES BACK TO ANCIENT ROME, EVIDENTLY. STRENGTH IN NUMBERS OR SOMETHING.
CONRAD, PLEASE...
THIS ISN'T ABOUT CORINNA. IT'S ABOUT MY *MOTHER.*
DRACULA *TURNED* HER. HE WANTS TO CONTROL HER, AND THROW TONIGHT'S VOTE.
HMM. SHE'S UP THERE RIGHT NOW, PERHAPS CORRUPTING THE BOARD AS WE SPEAK.
I SUPPOSE WE SHOULD GO UP.

CONRAD, I DON'T THINK YOU'RE TAKING THIS THREAT SERIOUSLY.
I CERTAINLY *AM.*
GOOD EVENING, EVERYONE!
MADAME CHAIRWOMAN, PLEASE ACCEPT MY APOLOGIES FOR BEING LATE.
I WAS TALKING WITH YOUR SON ABOUT SOME *ALARMING* RUMORS.
NOTHING TOO HORRIBLE, I HOPE.
WE HAVE ONLY TWO ITEMS ON THE AGENDA, BUT THEY WILL DETERMINE THE DESTINY OF THIS COMPANY.
FIRST UP, THE BUYOUT OFFER FROM THE HERMANNSTADT GROUP.
ALL IN FAVOR OF *REJECTING* THE OFFER, SAY AYE.

CAN I DENY YOU *NOTHING,* BROTHER?
AYE.
THE BOARD ECHOES HER. TURNING DOWN DRACULA'S BID.
AND IT'S THEN I REALIZE THE TRUTH. IT'S NOT *DRACULA* WHO TURNED HER.
CONRAD.
DO YOU WANT ME TO STOP HIM?
HE'LL BE BACK. HE HAS NOWHERE TO RUN.
BUT BEFORE WE BREAK OUT THE CHAMPAGNE, A FORMALITY.
ALL IN FAVOR OF *ACCEPTING* THE DEAL TO PURCHASE VERRAMETAL?

HOME IS NO LONGER A SANCTUARY.
AND MY FAMILY IS NO LONGER MY FAMILY. CONRAD HAS MADE SURE OF THAT.
PLEASE, STAY AS LONG AS YOU LIKE.
IT KILLS ME TO BURN IT ALL. BUT I HAVE TO TRAVEL LIGHT.
THE *CRUENTUS PACTUM* WILL HAVE TO DO.
IT'S MY ONLY WEAPON. AND NOT ONE I'M ABOUT TO GIVE UP--TO ANYONE.

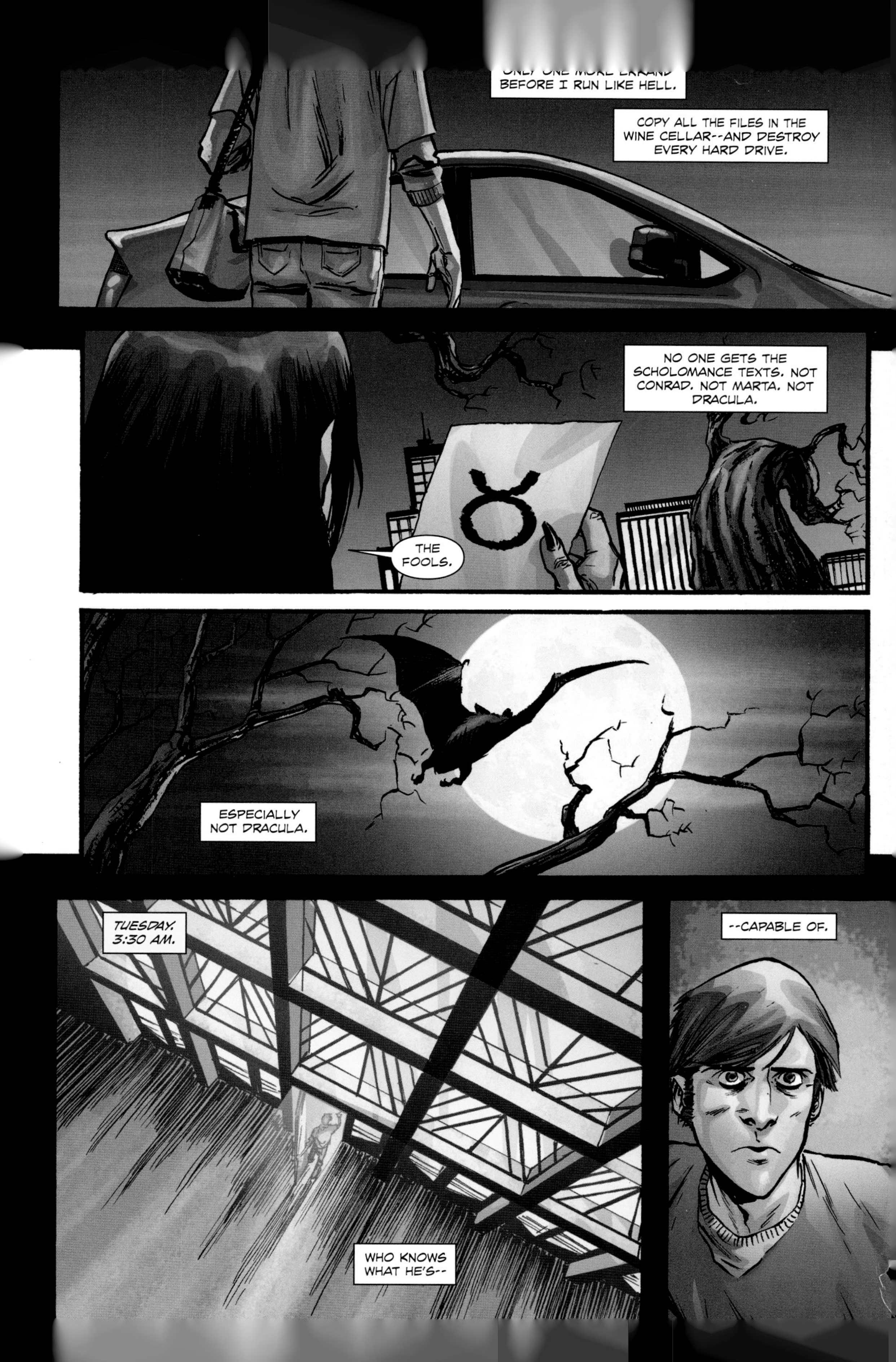
BEFORE I RUN LIKE HELL.
COPY ALL THE FILES IN THE WINE CELLAR--AND DESTROY EVERY HARD DRIVE.
NO ONE GETS THE SCHOLOMANCE TEXTS. NOT CONRAD. NOT MARTA. NOT DRACULA.
THE FOOLS.
ESPECIALLY NOT DRACULA.
TUESDAY. 3:30 AM.
WHO KNOWS WHAT HE'S--
--CAPABLE OF.

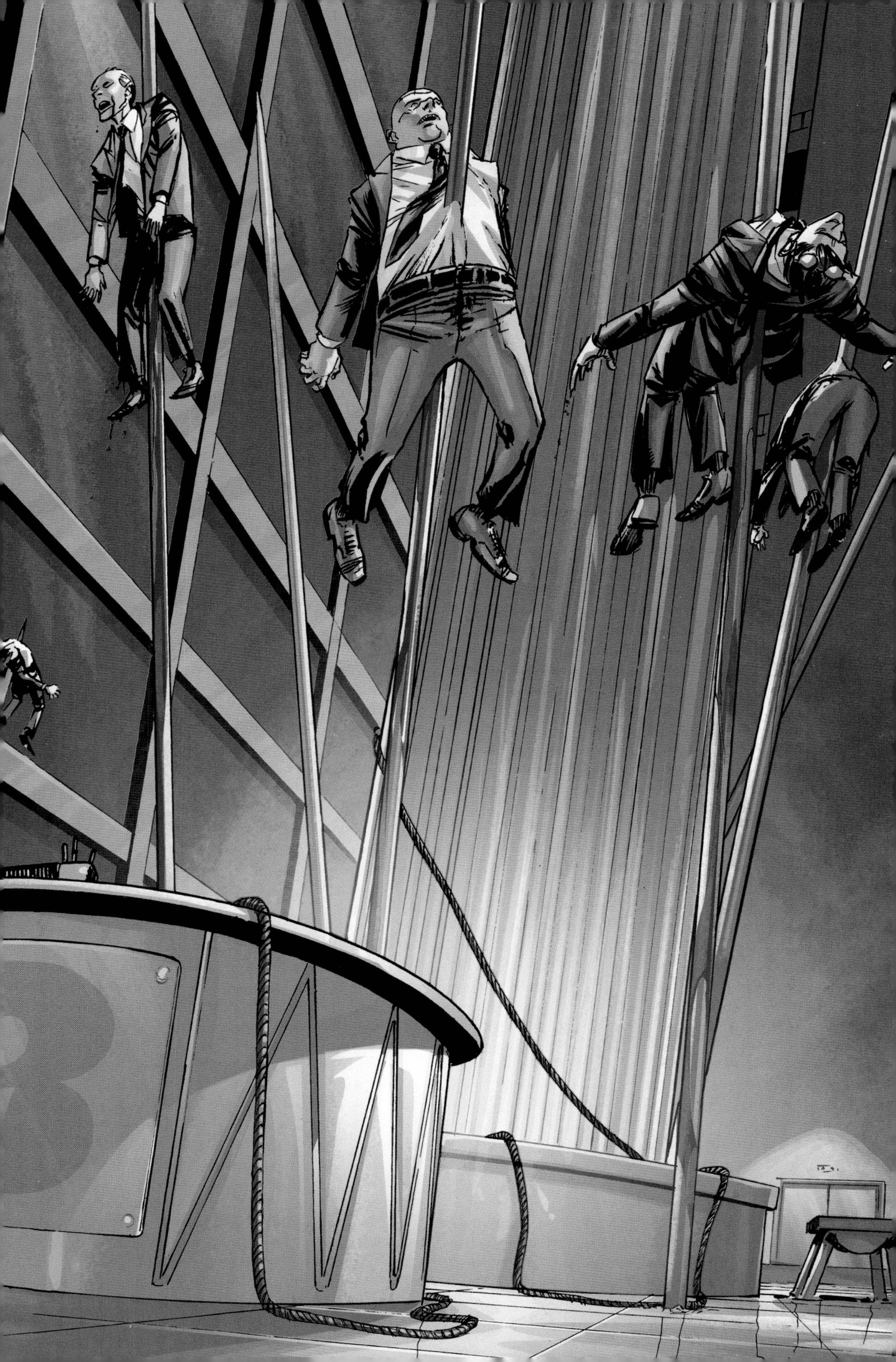

CONRAD. YOU HAVE TO COME TO B.I.
AND...I KNOW WHOSE SIDE I'M ON NOW.
I'M *IN.*
MARTA? IT'S ME, EVAN.
I'M IN.

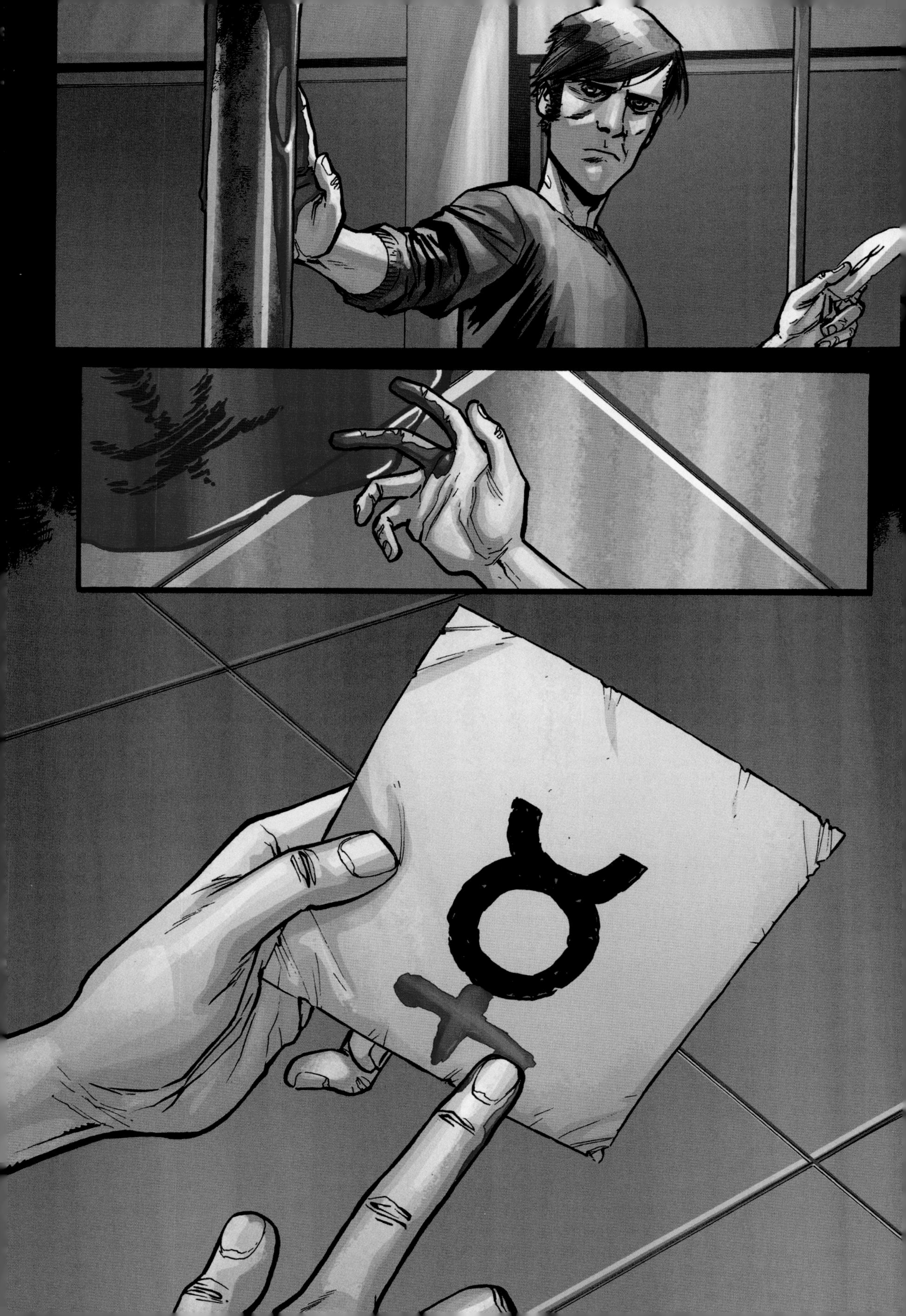

NO MORE RUNNING. NO MORE HIDING.
I'M IN.
HA HA HA HA HA!
ALL THE WAY IN.

COVER GALLERY

5: Ron Salas
colors: Archie Van Buren

6: Ron Salas
colors: Archie Van Buren

8: Ron Salas
colors: Darrin Moore

the art of
DRACULA

pages from sketch to finish
by Damian Couceiro
with colors by Stephen Downer

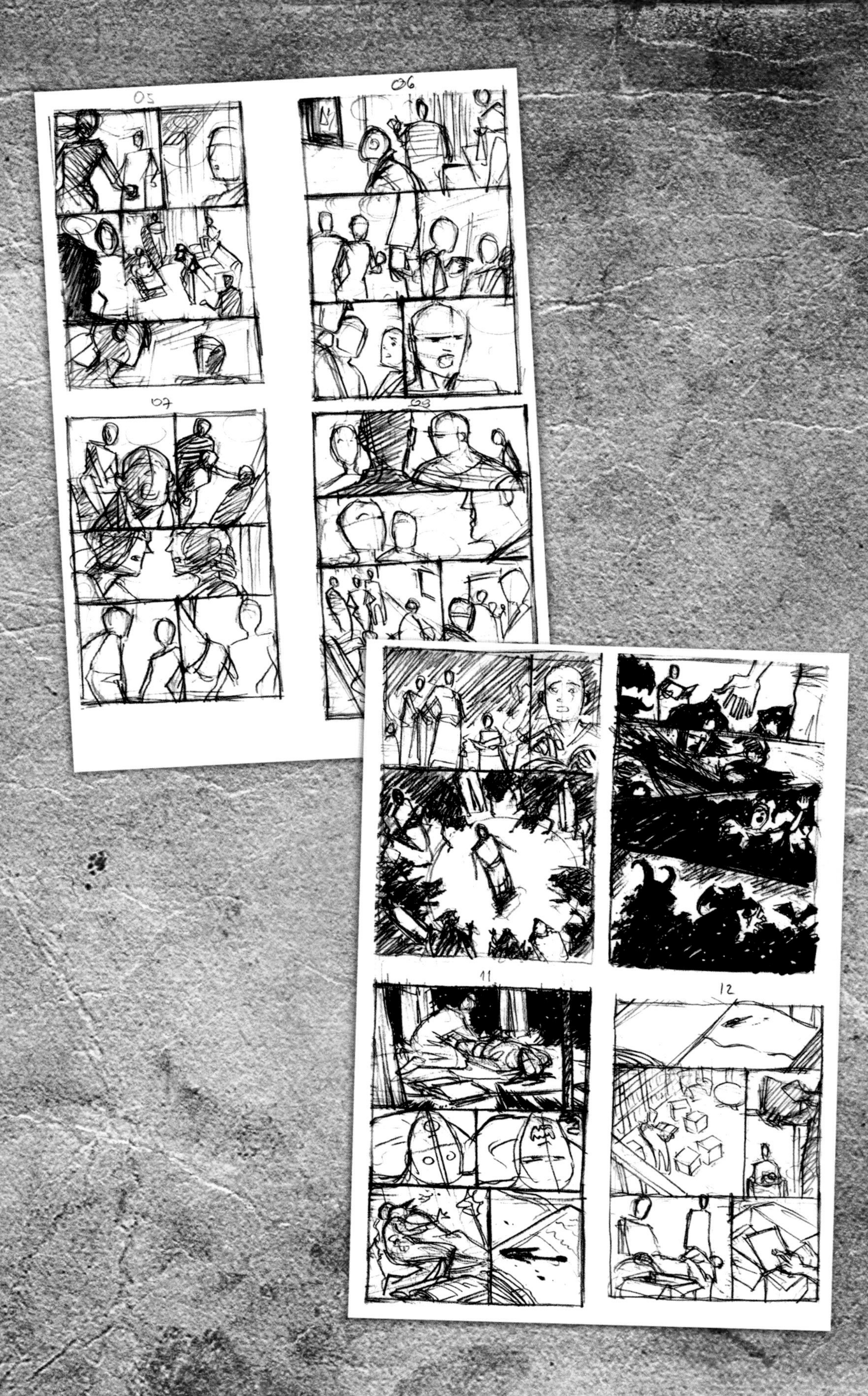
05
06
07
08
11
12

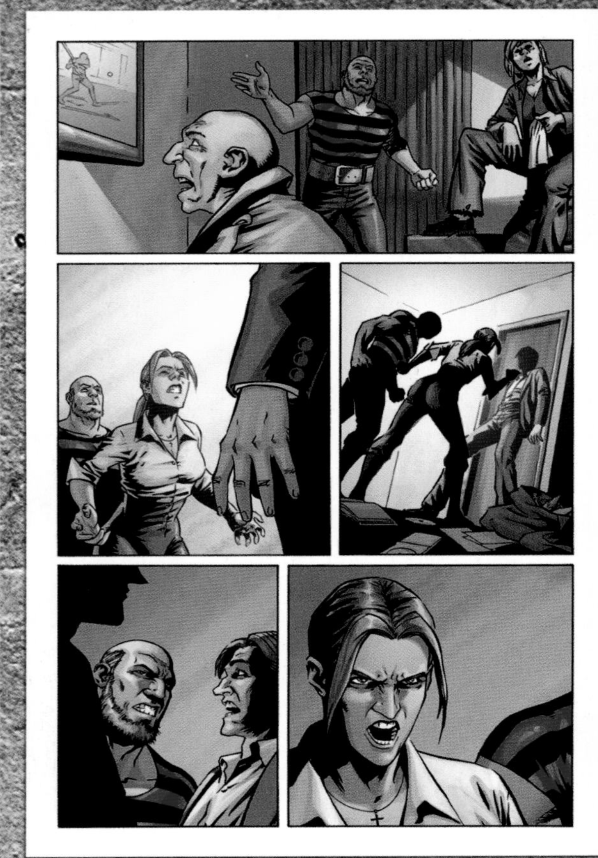

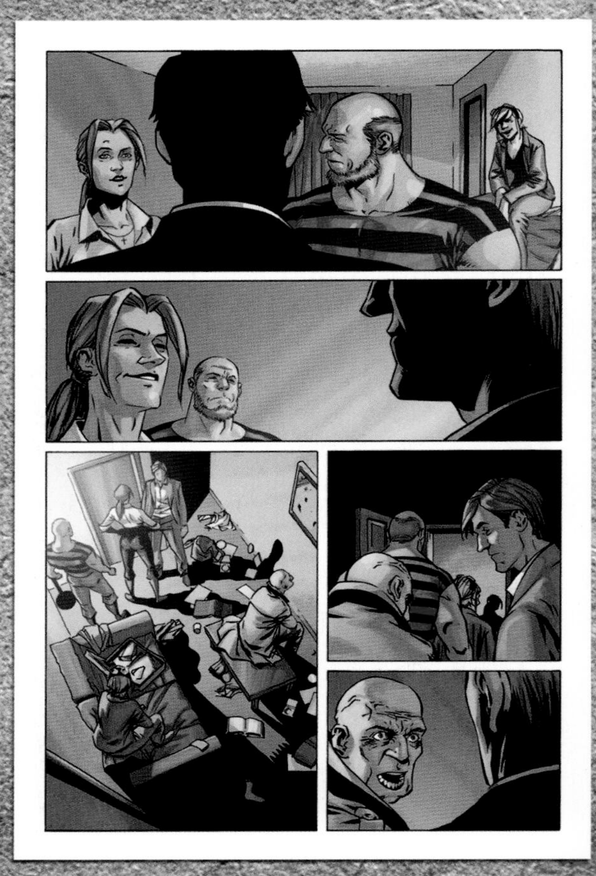

DRACULA

The Company of Monsters